William A. Crafts

State Railroad Commissions

William A. Crafts

State Railroad Commissions

ISBN/EAN: 9783744693707

Printed in Europe, USA, Canada, Australia, Japan

Cover: Foto ©ninafisch / pixelio.de

More available books at **www.hansebooks.com**

STATE RAILROAD COMMISSIONS.

TEN YEARS' WORKING OF THE MASSACHUSETTS

RAILROAD COMMISSION.

RAILROAD COMMISSION LAWS OF ALL THE

STATES THAT HAVE COMMISSIONS.

1883.

PUBLISHED BY THE RAILROAD GAZETTE,

73 BROADWAY, NEW YORK,

CONTENTS:

Page.

Ten Years' Working of the Massachusetts Railroad Commission.   3

State Railroad Commissions,   -   -   31

Laws of the Various States Establishing Railroad Commissions. 43

TEN YEARS' WORKING OF THE MASSACHUSETTS RAILROAD COMMISSION.

BY WM. A. CRAFTS.

The necessity for some governmental control and regulation of railroads has within a few years led many states of the Union to undertake that regulation through "railroad commissions." In a few of the states there had been for many years officers with that title, but with very limited powers, chiefly as to location or construction, which in other states were exercised by local authorities, or not exercised at all ; and their jurisdiction did not extend to the operations of railroads, or the relations of the corporations to the public. The immense extension of railroads since the civil war, the vast amount of business they do, their great importance in internal commerce of the country, and their tremendous power of aggregated wealth and monopoly have led the people who are independent upon them to seek some method of controlling them, compelling them to perform their duties as common carriers, and preventing extortion and unjust discrimination. General laws without some special officers to supervise their observance were found to be inoperative, and resort was had to commissions, with greater or less powers, as a means of enforcing statute laws, securing a compliance with the common law, and maintaining the rights of the public.

It is not the purpose of this article to discuss the subject of railroad commissions in general, but it may be observed, in passing, that in those states where they exist, while they may have corrected some abuses, they have not succeeded in introducing the millennium wherein the lion of "monopoly" shall lie down with the lamb of "popular rights." The failure of such commissions to accomplish all that might be accomplished may reasonably be attributed to some or all of the following causes :

(1) The non-reservation by the state of the power to amend or repeal the charters, and to subject the corporations to all subsequent general laws ; (2) the creation of commissions mainly to enforce popular prejudices shaped into crude and irrational laws, and to "regulate" that branch of the operation of railroads which cannot reasonably be subjected to fixed general rules ; (3) the making the commissionership too much a political office, subject to frequent change of incumbent, and the appointment of men prominent in the dominant party, who, if able enough, have not made the railroad problem a study, and bring only narrow ideas and prejudices to bear upon complex and difficult questions.

Among the railroad commissions of the several states, that of Massachusetts has alone acquired any considerable reputation beyond the limits of its own jurisdiction, and been recognized as a tribunal whose decisions were, in the main, founded in reason and equity. This is partly due to the conditions under which the board was established. The right of the state to control and regulate railroads had long been admitted and was reserved in granting concessions. The powers of the Commission were very limited, and its duties were very general ; so that it was obliged to survey the whole field of its possible operations and mark out for itself its course of action. It had to cope with no giant monopoly intrenched in "vested rights," such as existed in some other states. Moreover, it was fortunate in its composition, and in the ability and prudence which directed its action. Previous to the establishment of the present Board of Railroad Commissioners there had been two or three unsuccessful attempts to create such a commission. There was, however, no general demand for such legislation, and the railroad corporations were opposed to it. But in 1869 the railroad system of the state had become so extended and affected so many interests that public opinion favored, if it did not demand, that the state should exercise its right of control through some officer or board appointed for that purpose. The Boston Board of Trade and the manufacturing interests advocated such a measure, and it was supported by some influential parties interested in railroad property as a wiser method of exercising state control and shaping legislation than the ordinary process of making laws on subjects not thoroughly understood, to be admin·istered by the slow process of the courts. A bill was framed so moderate in its provisions that the Legislature, always jealous of delegating its authority, passed it with little opposition. The corporations were generally distrustful of any commission to have supervision of their interests, but the more prudent among their managers foresaw that if they successfully opposed this moderate measure there was danger that it would be followed by more stringent legislation, which it would be impossible for them to resist, and therefore they were content to give it a trial. The trial proved that the commission was a tribunal which could protect their interests as well as those of the public, and in the course of years they found that it saved them from not a little unwise legislation—unwise because it would prove unjust to the railroads and would not secure to the public the benefits it was designed to secure.

The law established a Board of Railroad Commissioners, to be composed of three competent persons to be appointed by the Governor, with the consent of the Council. The first appointees were to hold their office for one, two and three years respectively, and as each term expired one member was to be appointed annually for a term of three years. The board was to have a clerk, also appointed by the Governor, and no person in the employ or holding the stock of any railroad corporation of the state was eligible to either of the offices. This last provision was subsequently made more specific, if not more stringent.

The Commission was to have a general supervision of all railroads and street railways in the state, to examine them and keep themselves informed as to their condition and the manner in which they are operated with reference to the security and accommodation of the public, and to see that the several corporations comply with the terms of their charters and the laws of the commonwealth. In the case of a violation of any general law or neglect to comply with the terms of its charter by any corporation, the Commissioners were to give notice thereof in writing to the corporation, and if the violation or neglect continued after such notice, it was to be reported to the Attorney-General, for such proceedings as he might deem expedient.

When in the judgment of the commissioners " repairs are necessary upon any such railroad, or any
addition to the rolling stock, or any addition to
or change of the stations or station houses, or any
change in the rates of fares for transporting freight
or passengers, or any change in the mode of operating the road and conducting its business, is reasonable or expedient in order to promote the security,
convenience and accommodation of the public," they
were required to inform the corporation in writing
of the improvements and changes which they adjudge to be proper, and to report their proceedings
in their next annual report.

Complaints could be made by municipal authorities upon the petition of twenty or more legal voters.
Or if those authorities decline to make complaint,
they were to indorse their reasons for so doing on
the petition, which might then be presented to the
commissioners by the petitioners. If after hearing
the parties the commissioners adjudged the complaint well founded, they were to notify the corporation in the manner above mentioned.

Another duty of the Commission was to prescribe
the form of annual returns by the corporations, to
examine them and to require the correction of those
which were defective or erroneous, and to prepare
from them statistics for the information of the Legislature. It was also required to investigate the cause
of any accident on a railroad resulting in the loss of
life, and of such other accidents as it deemed proper.
An annual report to the Legislature was to cover all
the proceedings of the Commission, and to include
" such statements, facts and explanations as will disclose the actual working of the system of railroad

transportation in its bearing upon the business and prosperity of the Commonwealth, and such suggestions as to the general railroad policy of the Commonwealth, or as to any part thereof, or as to the condition, affairs or conduct of any of the railroad corporations as may seem appropriate."

Such was the scope of the prescribed duties and limited powers of the board, which are sufficiently comprehensive to include every branch of railroad management, and to impose upon the commissioners no very moderate amount of labor. But the manner in which those powers were to be exercised, and those duties were to be performed, it will be observed, was left in large measure to the "judgment" of the commissioners. In most cases they could only suggest or recommend such changes in modes of operation, or in rates and fares, as they deemed expedient. But, in that very want of direct power lay the real strength of the board, for it was obliged to weigh well its judgments and to give the reasons therefor, which might receive the support of public opinion. And behind it stood the Legislature, whose right to control the railroads was not disputed, and by whose authority recommendations not complied with could, if necessary, give to public opinion the force of statute law.

As a complement to the duties of the Commission, the corporations were required at all times to furnish the board, on request, with information concerning the condition, management and operation of their roads, with copies of all leases, contracts and agreements for transportation to which they were parties, and with the rates of transportation on their roads and joint rates on their own and connecting roads.

The first commissioners appointed under this act were James C. Converse, Edward Appleton and Charles Francis Adams, Jr., for three, two and one years respectively. Mr. Converse, who was the special candidate of the Boston Board of Trade, was a prominent merchant, who had been President of that Board. Before the civil war he had taken an active part in efforts to secure a more prompt forwarding and delivery of freight, and was supposed to represent the interests of shippers. Mr. Appleton was an experienced engineer, whose province was to advise the board in matters relating to construction, equipment and methods of operation. Mr. Adams, a lawyer by profession, had made the railroad problem a subject of special study, and had already earned a reputation by several able articles on railroad subjects. He had taken an active interest in the establishment of the Commission, and was the reputed author of the bill for its creation. Upon him devolved the consideration of all legal questions affecting the railroads and the public, and naturally the duty of preparing the reports of the board. Hence he gave direction to the inquiries and shaped the action of the Commission on all general questions.

Such was the *personnel* of the Commission first appointed. A distinguished member of the Legislature, in a speech opposing some measure relating to its duties, described the board as composed of "a merchant, an engineer and a—philosopher." The last title was given in good-natured derision, but as Mr. Adams had pursued the "scientific method" in his study of the railroad problem, the title was not altogether inappropriate. If he sometimes gener-

alized from insufficient facts, no one was more ready
to correct an error by further investigation.

Mr. Converse retired at the end of his term of
three years, and was succeeded by Francis M. Johnson, a successful merchant, a man of remarkably
clear intellect, a keen insight into questions of great
difficulty, and a thorough master of accounts. Mr.
Johnson was reappointed for a second term, for the
last six months of which failing health prevented
his attention to the duties, and he died soon after
the expiration of his term. His successor was Edward W. Kinsley, also a merchant, and a man
thoroughly acquainted with the wants of the traveling public, and quick to observe the management of
railroads as to equipment, accommodations and
facilities.

Mr. Appleton also retired at the expiration of his
term of two years, before the board had fairly
adapted itself to its position or adopted a policy, and
was succeeded by Albert D. Briggs, a civil engineer
and experienced bridge-builder ; a man whose judgment in respect to matters of construction and appliances was held in high esteem by railroad managers
and experts, and whose views on all general questions
of policy and management were intelligent, impartial and founded in reason. By successive reap-
pointments, he served till his death, in 1881.

Mr. Adams, by repeated appointments, served out
a decade, when he declined further service and was
succeeded by Judge Thomas Russell, the present
Chairman of the board, an able lawyer, quick of apprehension and of large experience in judicial and
executive office.

None of these appointments were in any sense

political, or made as rewards for party services. The
executive had honestly endeavored to select the men
best qualified for the position who were willing to
take it. And the board, not only in its organization,
but in its conduct, was far from being a political ma-
chine, contrary to the prophecies of some of the
opponents of its establishment.

Charged with rather numerous duties, prescribed
in general terms, and endowed with very limited
powers, the Commission had to determine for itself
the manner in which the objects aimed at should be
attained. The theory on which a board with such
limited power was created was, that it should be the
medium of concentrating public opinion and bring-
ing it to bear intelligently and persistently
upon abuses it was desirable to reform, without resorting to the power of the Legislature;
or, as Mr. Adams said in 1874, the Commission
was "simply a medium, a species of lens by
means of which the otherwise scattered and
powerless rays of public opinion could be concen-
trated to a focus, and brought to bear upon any
corporation." This result was to be brought about
by public hearings of complaints and a discussion of
the principles involved, or the true policy to be pursued. But at first, before the people had become ac-
customed to the Commission, and realized its possible
usefulness, complaints were few. To inspire the confidence of the public in it as a tribunal for the redress of grievances must necessarily be the work of
time. Meanwhile the board must educate public
opinion, and make itself known by the discussion of
various railroad questions which arose out of the
development of the system or the wants of the com-

munity. Its first efforts in this line were directed to the study of the railroad problem with reference to Massachusetts, the operation of the roads, and the manner in which they met the wants of the industries and commercial interests of the state.

At that time the Cunard steamships, which had plied between Liverpool and Boston for twenty-five years or more, had been withdrawn, and the foreign commerce of our domestic port had greatly diminished from its volume before the civil war. An attempt had been made, by means of a rebate on the rates for internal transportation of grain intended for export, to recover the lost prestige of the port, and to secure a regular return of the steamships, but it had met with only indifferent success. Under this aspect of affairs the Commission considered what the railroads might do for the interests of the state, and in its first annual report dwelt at some length on the various industries of Massachusetts, by which the commerce of Boston was to be maintained, and it was argued that the real interest of the city, as the commercial metropolis of New England, was not in becoming simply a port for the shipment of Western produce to Europe, so much as in being the distributing market for the numerous manufactures of the state, and of raw materials for those manufactures and food for the operatives. This would increase the coastwise commerce with other domestic ports, with the British provinces and the West Indies, and would lead to a substantial and permanent revival of more general foreign commerce. The change that had been going on in Massachusettts since the construction of the earlier railroads, from a commercial to a manufacturing community, and the policy of adapting the railroad system to this changed condition, were discussed in this first report with an ability which at once won for the Commission the respect of the corporations and the confidence of the public. Its argument, presented in various aspects, was that the true policy for such a community as that of Massachusetts is to foster its manufacturing industries, and to reduce the cost of production by all legitimate means, and thus promote its commercial interests also. The railroad system of such a community should, therefore, contribute to such a result by the carriage of raw materials, coal and food, at the lowest paying rates, and find its compensation in the transportation of the manufactures at rates more profitable from the nature of the service, but not excessive.

Unquestionably that is the true policy for a manufacturing state like Massachusetts, and that is the true province of its railroad system, as much now as in 1870. But of late years the competition of the chief seaports of the Union to secure a portion of the immense exports of grain and provisions to Europe has overshadowed the local interests. The great demand is for terminal facilities to receive and ship the products of the West, brought by the railroads often at scarcely paying rates, and docks for the accommodation of foreign steamers. While this business adds to the importance of the port and increases the amount of imports for distribution through the country, it contributes comparatively little in proportion to its volume, to the wealth of the city or the state. Meanwhile the rates for coal and raw materials, though reduced since 1870, are, for reasons that need not be here mentioned, much higher than those for grain brought for shipment to Europe.

It may be said, however, the Commission has always advocated the same policy of fostering local interests, though it may not have pressed it in so special a manner of late years while recognizing the demands of that general export trade which has contributed so greatly to the prosperity of the whole country. But it has repeatedly, in decisions concerning the coal rates on various roads, expressed the same views.

In later reports Mr. Adams, discussing the movement of freights East and West, described clearly the wars of rates, the combinations of the trunk lines, and the competition of the Atlantic ports with their respective lines of communication, and contributed largely to a knowledge of the facts concerning this immense business and a better comprehension of the actions and motives of managers of the rival routes. These discussions, while relating to a subject broader than state limits and addressed to a larger public, served also to show the relations of the railroad system of his own state to the greater system which extends through many states into distant territories and traverses hundreds of miles of the Dominion of Canada.

When the commission was created there was a general but indefinite demand from the commercial and manufacturing interests, and from a portion of the traveling public, that fares and rates should be reduced, and it was supposed by some that the Board would at once advocate specific reductions by legislation. Such action, however, was not recommended, and the Legislature then instructed the commission to examine the subject and report "by bill or otherwise." While the commissioners were earnest advocates of a reduction wherever reasonable, after a thorough examination of the subject they were satisfied that no general rule for rates could be adopted without doing injustice to some roads and some communities. The circumstances and conditions under which the ·various roads were constructed and operated were so different that what would be reasonable for one might be ruinous to another. To undertake to revise the tariff of each would be a work for which such a board was not competent, and could only be properly performed by those familiar with the business of the road and the wants and pursuits of the communities it served. Moreover, this system of governmental regulation of such matters was contrary to the theory on which the board was created, and the policy it aimed to carry out. The report of the Commission on these instructions of the Legislature, which was opposed to the policy adopted in some other states and adverse to the popular notions, was exhaustive and able, and for a time at least settled the policy of the state in its supervision of railroads. By this decision the corporations and the public were saved from controversies and continued hostility, which would have been prejudicial to the interests of both.

The problem, therefore, to the solution of which the Commission addressed its consideration was how to secure a reduction of rates and increased facilities and accommodations for the public, or, in other words, how the roads could best be made to promote the interests of the state. An earnest recommendation to the managers of the several roads to revise and reduce their tariff rates was complied with to some extent by a few, and whenever complaints were presented the board made specific recommendations which were seldom disregarded. But something more cogent and more general seemed to be demanded, and the Commission sought tentatively some plan which might have something of the force of legislation while leaving the roads to consult their own interests under circumstances which would necessarily lead to a reduction of rates and a better accommodation of the public.

The first measure of general policy directed to this end was the suggestion that the state adopt as an experiment the system of government ownership and operation of a part of the railroad system as a competitor and example to the roads owned by the corporations. This system prevailed in Belgium, where it had proved a success, as was shown in a report made by the Assistant Secretary of the English Board of Trade and laid before a Parliamentary committee. To carry this plan into effect the Commission proposed that the state should take the Fitchburg Railroad under its reserved rights or by purchase and operate it in the interests of the public, who should have the benefit of reduced rates to the extent that the earnings were in excess of the operating expenses, renewals and interest on the cost. It was proposed to take the Fitchburg road because it was wholly within the state and perhaps because it was a comparatively moderate experiment. But unless the plan was extended further it is not easy to see how the alleged advantages of partial state ownership could be realized, for the road was then as little of a competing route as any in the state. It is probable, however, that the Commission even then looked to an extension of

the system such as it subsequently proposed. The
suggestion was first made in 1871 ; its adoption was
again urged in the next annual report, and in 1873
the board proposed that the state should acquire not
only the Fitchburg, but the Vermont & Massachusetts road, and thus, with the Troy & Greenfield,
which it already owned, should have a line through
the length of its territory. It was also proposed to
acquire the Massachusetts Central road, the construction of which was scarcely begun. But even
with this line of road, extending through the length
of the state, the system would scarcely be analogous
to the Belgian system, where the state roads reach
competitive points in all parts of the kingdom, and
to accomplish anything for the Massachusetts railroad system it would be necessary that the state
should also own lateral roads or branches to compete
to any considerable extent with the corporations.

Mr. Adams made an elaborate and able argument
in support of this proposition before the legislative
committee on railroads, reviewing the various attempts made in other states and in England to secure
low and equal rates, and maintaining that direct
legislation was ineffectual to prevent combination—
the certain result of private competition—but that
state ownership of one through line would make
combination impossible, and, therefore, competition
certain. Moreover, the state road by reducing rates
on its whole line would attract thither manufacturing
interests, and similar interests on other lines would
raise a clamor for an equal reduction that could not
be ignored.

But whatever might be the theoretical advantages
of this system as a regulator of the railroads of the

corporations, and whatever its success in Belgium, it was open to the fundamental objection that it is no part of the functions of a republican form of government to engage in any commercial or industrial enterprises, and that under such a form of government, liable to frequent changes, the management of a state road would be neither efficient nor economical. While the plan which the Commission had in view would have in a measure met these objections, and divorced the management of the road as much as possible from politics, the proposition did not meet with favor from the Legislature. It was too formidable a project, too large and costly an experiment. In view of the experience of the state with the Hoosac Tunnel, and the large outlay required for terminal facilities for the through business of this line, it is certainly no matter for regret that the proposition failed. The idea was abandoned and the commissioners, never unwilling to recede from an untenable position, did not again suggest it, even if they did not very soon entirely change their views.* The discussion, however, had not been without advantage to the public. Discussion, indeed, in this case as in some others, was the object of the Commission rather than to force the adoption of the policy advocated. By it the public was familiarized with different phases of the railroad problem, and its opinions were more intelligently formed.

Meanwhile the Commission continued its recommendations to the railroads to reduce their rates,

---

* In 1874 Mr. Adams, in one of a course of lectures at the Lowell Institute, expressed the opinion that the best method of regulation under our American form of government—and for the present, at least, better than any system of continental Europe—is through the force of intelligent public opinion, the theory on which the Massachusetts Commission was created and conducted.

and supported its views by cogent arguments,
diffusing a better knowledge of the operation of railroads and giving direction to public opinion so as to
produce an effect upon the corporations. The
railroad managers, while generally receiving the
recommendations with respect, and in some instances making concessions, replied that a reduction such as was suggested would be in-
jurious to them, alleging that with existing rates
they only pay operating expenses and fair
dividends. In their investigations of this matter of
operating expenses, the commissioners, at the out-
set, found that it was impossible to obtain from the
returns, as then made, any satisfactory results, and
that, for the purposes of comparison, the returns of
the various roads were simply absurd. The method
of keeping accounts differed widely, and the items of
operating expenses were not limited by any common
rule, but embraced expenditures for permanent
improvements according to the policy of each management. Moreover, the returns were often made
with evident want of care and thorough book-keeping, the return of a road for one year upon comparison with that of the preceding year sometimes
showing marked discrepancies. The form of returns
was improved, and a careful and laborious analysis
was made of each report and corrections required.
By this means somewhat more satisfactory returns
were obtained. Still they were not what was desired for the purposes of comparison by students of
the railroad problem.

The board then recommended that a uniform system of accounts should be required by law. Uniformity and publicity, it was argued, would lead to

a solution of the cost of transportation on the several roads, and the average cost would make a just comparison of different modes of operation possible and supervision intelligent. The public would thus be enabled to understand better the financial condition of the corporations and the reasonableness of rates and fares, and the railroad managers could better see in what direction they could improve their methods.

The Legislature, whose authority was necessary to enforce such a measure, adopted this recommendation, and a law was passed authorizing the board to prescribe a system of accounts which every corporation operating a railroad was required to follow. Under the provisions of this act the Commission appointed an experienced railroad accountant as Supervisor of Railroad Accounts and Returns, and by a conference with the auditors of the principal roads of the state a system was agreed upon to which all the corporations were required to conform.

To secure more completely the advantage of such a system it was desirable that it should be adopted in the neighboring states with the railroads of which those of Massachusetts were connected and were doing a joint business. Accordingly the Commissioners of adjoining states, including the State Engineer of New York, were invited to join in recommending the adoption of such a uniform system. The Commission had repeatedly dwelt upon the subject in its reports, and had urged it with so much force, as the first requisite and basis of any intelligent supervision or reform, that it received attention in other states, and at a convention of the commissioners of a number of states, east and west, a committee of experts prepared a general system of railroad book-keeping, and a more concise return, which was substantially adopted in most of the states represented in the convention. This system left the details of book-keeping and accounts to the corporations as they should consider best adapted to their business and mode of operation, and required only that the operating expenses and expenditures for permanent improvements should be uniformly carried to certain general accounts.

One of the special duties of the board was to investigate railroad accidents, with a view to ascertaining the cause of and responsibility for each, in order that, by legislation or otherwise, similar accidents might be prevented, or at least rendered less frequent. Early in the history of the Commission occurred the terrible Revere disaster on the Eastern Railroad, in which thirty-one persons were killed and sixty or more were injured. At that time many of the appliances and methods of operation now in general use had been adopted to only a very limited extent, and in this respect the railroads of Massachusetts, though generally operated with care, were not abreast with those of some other states. The telegraph was scarcely used ; the block system was unknown ; train brakes had not been tried ; the discipline of employés was lax ; loose couplings and weak platforms were conducive to telescoping in case of collision or derailment ; crude and ineffectual signals were still in use. The accident at Revere awoke the managers of the roads of large traffic to the risk they incurred not only of sacrificing human life but of draining their treasuries by the payment of damages.

The commissioners, having thoroughly investigated the accident, took advantage of the aroused sense of danger and responsibility to earnestly recommend improvements in the methods of operation, the use of new appliances and a revision and a thorough enforcement of rules. Not only was the Revere accident investigated, but the board inquired into the causes of other train accidents, drawing from them lessons of value at that juncture. In this connection it did a good work in refuting the charge, then quite common, and still supposed by some to be well-founded, that such an accident as that at Revere could not occur on any European road, and that train accidents in this country are both much more frequent and more fatal than in Europe. By official reports and statistics it was shown that neither of these assertions was true, and, so far as the Massachusetts roads were concerned, that the proportion of passengers killed and injured to the whole number carried during a period of ten years was smaller than in Great Britain, and about the same as in Belgium.

With the co-operation of the managers of some of the principal roads, a new and more efficient code of rules was agreed upon, and its adoption recommended to all the roads in the state—a recommendation that was complied with so far as applicable to their traffic. The Commission further urged upon the managers a better construction of passenger cars, the use of train brakes operated from the locomotive, a more general use of the telegraph, the adoption of the block system, and other improvements which had been tested elsewhere. These recommendations were received at first with more or less doubt of their feasibility or wisdom by the managers, but

gradually many of them were introduced, and probably at a much earlier date than they would have been
had not the Commission exerted a constant influence
in that direction.

To the Eastern Railroad the result of the accident
and the investigation was a change of management
and a more progressive policy. The new management adopted all the improvements recommended by
the Commission—better car construction, Miller plat-
form and couplers, train brakes, an electric block system and more perfect discipline of employés. Without doubt, the Revere disaster was the primary
cause of the financial difficulties in which the company afterward became involved; but it could have
safely borne the heavy damages and the large expense of its extensive improvements, had not the
ambitious enterprise of the management led it into
schemes of extension and connections which proved
disastrous. The traveling public, however, derived
no small advantage from the liberal action of the
Eastern Railroad, for in its improvements it was an
example which public opinion demanded should be
followed by other roads.

One of the functions of the Commission was to
give its aid and advice in matters of legislation
besides those initiated by itself. On all general
propositions concerning railroads coming before the
Legislature by petition or order of inquiry, the committees having those subjects in charge consulted
the board, and many matters were specially referred
to it for report as to the expediency of legislation
and the framing of bills. In this province, which
might perhaps be considered its most important one,
the Commission has rendered great service, both to

the public and the corporations, by preventing crude and unwise legislation, and advocating with cogent reasons such laws as in their judgment would promote the interests of the people and the railroads. By its efforts a general law for the incorporation of railroad companies was passed, and the legislative committees were relieved of much labor and saved from a waste of time in considering the projects of parties who desired to obtain "strategic charters" and competitive routes on paper, as well as *bona fide* and legitimate enterprises. It also secured general provisions of law for the settlement of many other questions which else would have required special legislation in numerous cases.

One result of the conferences and discussions with the legislative committees was to convince legislators that such a Commission was a better tribunal for hearing and determining many questions relating to railroads than the General Court could possibly be. Hence, while the board never sought to extend its jurisdiction, its powers and duties were from time to time enlarged till they are so interwoven with the railroad system of the state that if the Commission were abolished a complete revision of the general railroad law would be required.

While aiming by general recommendations to secure improvement in the management of railroads, and to promote the common interests of the public by increased facilities, lower rates and safer transportation, the Commission was designed especially to be a tribunal for redressing grievances, and parties who had such grievances were invited to present complaints or petitions for a hearing. At first such complaints were comparatively few, but as the

board became better known as an impartial tribunal
which recognized the obligations as well as the
rights of the corporations, the applications for redress became more frequent. Parties who had just
cause of complaint were satisfied, for although the
Commission had power only to "recommend," the
grounds of its recommendations were stated so for-
cibly that with the weight of public opinion in their
favor there was hardly one but was promptly complied with by the railroad managers in terms or by
some arrangement equally satisfactory to the petitioners. On the other hand, the corporations found
that unjust complaints and unreasonable petitions
were dismissed with no less cogent arguments, and
that the Commission was in effect a buffer to moderate the shock of collision between them and an ex-
acting or indignant public. Being neither politic-
ians, nor partisans, nor representatives of any
"league" or special interest, the commissioners thoroughly examined all questions submitted to them,
and the conclusions at which they arrived by their
impartiality won the respect if not always the entire
acquiescence of all parties. Moreover they were
men whom no one dared to approach with a corrupt
purpose.

The reports of the hearings and decisions printed
with the annual report of the board comprise but a
small part of the cases actually presented and
settled. Many complaints made verbally or by
letter were adjusted by an informal interview or
correspondence with railroad officials, and occasion-
ally petitioners were forced to admit that what they
asked was unreasonable. Moreover, railroad managers not infrequently applied to the Commission

for advice in matters affecting their rights and obligations, and this was given in a like informal manner and with good results.

To keep themselves informed of the condition of the railroads, the commissioners made annual, and when necessary more frequent, examinations of every road in the state. When the board was first established it was supposed by railroad managers and the public that these examinations would be mere junketing excursions, comprising a good deal of pleasure with very little work ; but the commissioners soon corrected this impression, so far at least as railroad officials were concerned, and the examinations became laborious and thorough. Track and road bed, every bridge and station, shops and terminals were inspected in company with the experts of the road, and criticism and commendation were impartially expressed, and advice and suggestions were offered and in most cases were promptly followed. Sometimes experts were employed, and in special cases sharp reports were made, demanding immediate improvements to secure the safety of travelers.

After a service of ten years Mr. Adams retired from the board. The experience of those ten years tested the value of a railroad commission established on a basis which he had advocated, and whose policy and proceedings he had in the main directed. It is not to be inferred, however, that the other members of the Commission were mere ciphers in determining its action. Those who served the greater part of that period heartily co-operated with him ; all important matters were freely discussed, and after an interchange of views the Commission almost invariably acted as a unit.

And what had the Commission accomplished? In general, it had by its reports and decisions contributed largely to a better knowledge of the various railroad questions that arose, and had given direction to public opinion so as to exert a constant influence upon railroad managers, and make it a force in securing reforms, while at the same time it had brought about a better understanding of the mutual relations of the corporations and the public. It had, moreover, established itself in the confidence of the people as a tribunal for the redress of grievances and the correction of abuses.

Specifically, it had held the railroad companies to obedience to the laws; it had procured the passage of a general law for the charter of railroad companies, to the great relief of the Legislature, and it had successfully advocated the passage of other laws for the benefit alike of the public and the corporations, while it had also with equal success opposed unwise and ill-considered legislation. Without authority to regulate rates or prevent discrimination, its recommendation had been followed in many instances by a voluntary reduction by the companies, and equal terms to all parties for like service. It had exposed fraud and mismanagement in several schemes for the construction of new roads, and had secured a uniformity of accounts and returns which made its statistics of value to interested parties, and rendered the detection of fraudulent or unwise management more easy. It had investigated accidents and fixed the responsibility therefor, whether on the corporations or their agents, and it had hastened the introduction of· a better equipment and the adoption of appliances for the safety of travelers. It had secured better accommodations and facilities for many places, and had redressed many grievances of individuals and communities. And it had accomplished its work without creating or encouraging any violent antagonism between the people and the corporations, but, on the contrary, had rendered their relations more harmonicus and satisfactory. Certain rules of action were early laid down by the Commission and were consistently followed, and sound principles applied to successive decisions came to be well established in its administration, and those decisions were in most cases accepted as final.

With such results it may safely be asserted that the Massachusetts Commission has been a success and a benefit alike to the railroad corporations and the people, and the state has wisely continued it, gradually enlarging its powers and adding to its duties. And not till its character is essentially changed will there be any general desire to resort to a different method of supervision and control.

Out of the complex system of railroads extending through the states of the Union broader questions arise which are beyond the jurisdiction of a sta'e Commission. Whether those questions can be satisfactorily settled through intelligent supervision and the application of sound principles by a tribunal of like character to that we have described, but with a wider jurisdiction, is a problem that need not be here discussed. But within state lines there would seem to be no reason why tribunals like the Massachusetts Railroad Commission may not redress many grievances, secure increased facilities and accommo-

dations, and bring about more harmonious relations
between the railroads and the people.

NOTE.—The foregoing paper was intended to cover only the first ten
years of the Massachusetts Railroad Commission. During that period
its character, purpose and policy were established, and it entered upon
its second decade a tribunal having the respect and confidence of the
public and the railroad interests, and capable of dealing intelligently
with any question coming within its jurisdiction. During the present
year there have been changes in the composition of the board, and the
original and well considered theory of selection has been disregarded
by the present executive. What will be the result of this experiment
with the Commission remains to be seen.

STATE RAILROAD COMMISSIONS.

[From the Railroad Gazette of Aug. 24, 1883.]

There have been "railroad commissions" in some of the states from a very early date. In 1855 there was one in New York which issued a report in two large volumes, one giving the profiles and align‑ments of all the railroads in the state—valuable in‑formation which is not now obtainable in any other publication. But for the most part until after the war there was no railroad commission which was much felt or widely known in the community. But within the last 15 years not only have commissions been established in many states, but they have at‑tracted much attention, investigated many questions that arise in the relations of the railroads to the public, published voluminous reports, some of which contain carefully compiled and valuable statistics, and in a few states exercised a very considerable in‑fluence on the conduct of railroad business. At this time there is a railroad commission in every Northern state west of Colorado except New Jersey, Pennsylvania, Indiana and Nebraska; and in the South, where the institution is but a few years old, Virginia, South Carolina, Georgia, Alabama, Tennes‑see and Kentucky have commissions. The public has come to look upon them as a means by which it can in some degree regulate and restrain corporate manage‑ment and prevent abuses from which it might suffer This view evidently gains ground, for while in 1870 there were but two states, Ohio and Massachusetts, which had railroad commissions which attracted any public attention, since that time they have been established in nearly every Northern state, and nearly every year a new one is established—one in Kansas and one in Tennessee this year, one in New York last year, one in Alabama in 1881, etc. Moreover, in many of the states which have no commission there is a nearly successful attempt to establish one at every session of the legislature, as in Nebraska, Colorado, Texas and Indiana very recently.

What is the nature and the operation of this comparatively new but widely prevailing and growing institution? The workings of one of the oldest and by far the most influential of them, the Massachusetts Commission, was recently told in these columns by Mr. Wm. A. Crafts. This sets forth the authority, working, and the achievements of one type of railroad commissions, and the one which has been most regarded in the legislation for the commissions established since 1870. It is the best single answer to the question : What is a railroad commission?

Our state railroad commissions, however, are not all alike, by any means. The summary of the railroad commission laws of the several states, which follows, shows marked differences in their powers and functions.*

The first of the state railroad commissions now existing which made any noise in the world is the Ohio Commission, whose first report was for the year 1867. Gen. George B. Wright, afterwards President of the Atlantic & Great Western, and, later, Receiver of the Indiana, Bloomington &

---

*"Ten Years of a Railroad Commission." *The Railroad Gazette* p. 367, June 8, and p. 388, June 15, 1883.

Western, was the first Commissioner there, held the office for several years, and made some investigations of and reports upon matters of practical importance and public interest which received some attention at the time.

The prototype of the modern railroad commission, however, is undoubtedly the Massachusetts Commission, whose doings Mr. Crafts has so well sketched. It was fortunate in having on it a publicist of great independence and force of character as well as intelligence, who made a serious study of the relations of the railroads to the public—a question which scarcely any one in this country had studied profoundly—and who, moreover, was gifted with a clear and forcible style, which made his reports readable. Mr. Adams' essays on "The Railroad Problem," given yearly in the Massachusetts reports, came at a time, too, when there was a great outcry in the Northwest against the railroads, and this was another reason why they were generally read.

Considering what the early Northwestern commissions were, it might be said that Mr. Adams' essays had very little immediate effect, except to cause the legislatures to call "railroad commissions" the tribunals which they set up to regulate or restrain the railroads in their relations to the public. But, in fact, these bodies usually had substantially all the powers of the Massachusetts Railroad Commission, and differed from it chiefly in having a great deal more besides. There has been and still is a very general misapprehension as to the work of the best known railroad commissions, and to-day the prevailing belief doubtless is that the Massachusetts, Michigan, Wisconsin, Minnesota and Iowa commissions have power to say what the railroads may charge for their services. This misapprehension extends to the British Railway Commission, which is of more recent creation than many of our state commissions* and has very little in common with them except its name. Yet the leading New York newspapers when it was proposed to establish a railroad commission of the Massachusetts type in New York argued in favor of the proposition that the "Railway Commission" had worked well in England, which is about as apropos as to cite the usefulness of the Court of Arbitration in New York, or the distinguished services of Mr. Albert Fink as a "Commissioner," as evidence in favor of a Railroad Commission.

Without going into the history of the railroad commissions of this country, but considering only their present development, we may distinguish three different kinds. The oldest of these, but the least known, because it has had little to do or has done little, is a body appointed to do some special or formal work, or intrusted with powers of inspection or the like, which it exercises at its own discretion, but actually scarcely exercises at all, or so little that its existence is hardly felt. For instance, there was a so-called "railroad commission" in Tennessee in 1870 with power to sell or lease railroads which were in default to the state for loans made them before the war—a temporary purpose. In Arkansas not long after the war, when the state was loaning its bonds to new railroads, three state officers were made a "railroad commission" to hear and decide upon applications for state aid. In New Jersey the Comptroller, Treasurer and Commissioner of Railroad

---

* The act establishing it was passed in July, 1873.

Taxation form a "railroad commission" to appraise
the property of railroad companies which do not
make returns of such property. None of these have
any of the regulating or inspecting powers which are
generally characteristic of state railroad commissioners.

The older commissions which are least known and
have usually been least active seem to have been
originally almost solely inspectors, who exercised
their functions and made their reports at their discretion, and usually did very little in either direction. Several of these have made much fuller reports since the Massachusetts Commission became so
widely known and influential, and have had their
powers and duties increased. All the New England
commissions (and there is one in each state) were
of this character originally, we believe, including
the Massachusetts Commission, or a Massachusetts
Commission. In Maine the commissioners actually
executed inspecting functions to the point that many
years ago they ordered train service suspended on a
line until certain repairs should be made, resulting
in the abandonment of the road, we believe.
In New Hampshire the duties imposed on the
commissioners by law could only be properly performed by a corps of experts, the result of which
has been, of course, that their reports have been
chiefly formal and apparently have had very little
effect. The Vermont Commission is less heard of
than any other, and its reports, if it makes any, apparently do not usually come to light. The Connecticut Commission of late years has been an active
body and issued a voluminous report. But the New
England states are too small for any one of them to

contain the whole of an important railroad system ; only Massachusetts has an important railroad terminus ; and to this day New England railroads are mostly small, and its traffic different in character from that of most other parts of the country. Massachusetts, having the terminus of a true trunk line, has been the only fair field for the exhibition of what we may call national railroad phenomena.

The Ohio Commission, the oldest of the Western railroad commissions, was probably based on the earlier New England commissions. It was, and indeed still remains, primarily an inspecting authority, designed to secure the safety of the railroads—to reduce liability to accident. But it was, with General Wright as the first Commissioner, active in its first years, and made reports which attracted some attention before the Massachusetts Commission was well known. At present its powers apparently do not differ greatly from those of the Massachusetts Commission, but its reports have had little discussion of value on the relations of the railroads to the public.

The distinguishing feature of the Massachusetts type of commission is not its authority, but its want of authority. Its duties are chiefly to investigate complaints, to report on these and on all other railroad affairs which affect the community and *to make recommendations* to the Legislature. How great an influence has been exerted in this way with regard to rates and accommodations by a body which has no authority to dictate rates or accommodations is well shown in Mr. Crafts' paper and has been insisted upon with great force by Mr. Adams in the Massachusetts reports and before committees of Congress and elsewhere. Of the way in which this influence is exerted we will have more to say hereafter.

The third variety of American railroad commission was born in the Northwest of the "Granger" agitation about 1870, and is purely an American product; but its home is now chiefly in the South and not in the Northwest, where some of the original commissions have been greatly modified. This is the commission with authority to dictate rates, or in charge of the execution of laws which limit rates closely. The first were in Illinois and Wisconsin, and the constitutionality of the laws giving such power over rates was contested to the last, with the result that it was affirmed. Afterward the California Commission was established, with almost unlimited powers in this direction. Iowa once had such a commission, but like Wisconsin has changed it for one of the Massachusetts type ; but the Illinois Commission still has authority to dictate rates, and so has the more recent Missouri Commission, and the Kansas Commission has authority which gives it power to declare, after investigation of a complaint that rates are excessive or unjust, what are reasonable rates in that case, which will be *prima facie* evidence in the courts of what is a reasonable charge—a greatly modified authority over rates. In the South, the Georgia Commission has almost absolute authority over rates. The South Carolina Commission, which until this year was of the Massachusetts type, has been given power over rates similar to that of the Georgia Commission. The Alabama Commission, not yet three years old, has power something like the power of "homologation" of the French Minister of

Public Works ; all tariffs of rates must be submitted
to it, and are legal only if it approves.

We have said that the commission with authority
to dictate rates is a purely American product. Not
but that great powers over rates are exercised by
governments elsewhere, and indeed in almost all
European states except England. But such arbi-.
trary power is exercised nowhere out of the United
States. In France, the authorities can refuse to per-
mit new schedules of rates, and limits of charges are
fixed by law ; but the government cannot make a
schedule of rates and impose it upon the railroads,
and, in fact, nothing is done without consultations
and negotiations between the companies and the authorities. In France, too, the government is represented, not by citizens without any special knowledge of railroad business, but by a large and highly-
trained corps of experts, from which the railroads
themselves obtain their chief officers. In Germany,
changes in rates by the authorities, in the days when
the corporation railroad system was still so extensive that the state railroads could not dictate
rates nearly everywhere, as they can now, were
made only after investigations lasting for
many months, during which there were scores of
conferences with the railroad officers, state and
company, with commercial bodies, associations of
railroads, etc., reports of committees and experts
covering all points and interests, and the utmost
pains to avoid injury to the interests of the railroads, or any special industry, as well as the community at large. We have before us as we write a
report of the proceedings and resolutions of "the
Standing Committee on Rates of the German Rail-

roads, and the Representatives of Freight Shippers"
on modifications of the general basis of the German
freight taiiff—a volume of 240 pages, giving reports
of meetings, held from Nov. 13, 1878, to Feb. 13
1880, in which modifications of classification alone
were chiefly considered ; and all changes made there
have been trifling compared with the sweeping ones
introduced by some of our state commissions with
but the slightest consultation with those who perform
the service for which the commissions fix the price.
Further, the authority, whatever it may be, which
European states exercise over railroads was one of
the conditions of their establishment, and was so
understood. Again, as against the control (more
apparent in matters affecting construction, equipment and operation than in rates) which the
European states exercise over railroads must be set
the protection which they afford. An American
company may construct a railroad through a territory which it is abundantly able to serve alone,
receive little or no interest on its capital for years,
while the country is growing and its traffic developing, and when the business has become large enough
to give it ample support and begins to pay interest
for the previous years, new lines may be built on
either side which will indefinitely postpone the day
when the investors will receive their reward. On
the continent of Europe this is not permitted. The
railroad is required to afford adequate service, and
its charges are limited (though not so much so but
that dividends of 12 and 14 per cent. are often
made), but it is protected in its territory. But our
commissions with authority to prescribe rates have
no authority to prevent the construction of parallel

railroads, and the community in states where such
commissions exist are most eager to have such competing lines established. The rates, in fact, are there
established by one party only—the buyer. The
Commission represents him and him only. The
seller is left without any voice in fixing the wages
for which he must work.

Where commissions with power to dictate have
been preferred to commissions of the Massachusetts type with power only to investigate, report and
recommend, the reason given for the preference
usually is that corporations have no regard to recommendations, and that nothing short of an order
which the sheriff can enforce will avail to restrain
railroad abuses. Mr. Adams and Mr. Crafts have
shown very clearly that the power to investigate
and report and recommend has in fact been effective
in Massachusetts. But less credit than it deserves
has been given to the effectiveness of this type of
commission, because the public has not clearly seen
why it is effective. It is not by any means because
corporations have feelings which are peculiarly sen-
sitive to public opinion, but because they know that
behind public opinion, when formulated after
thorough investigation by a capable and independent
tribunal, there lies a power which it is impossible to resist; and that if they take no heed to recommendations
made by such a body with a full statement of the reasons for them, they are likely to be compelled by law
to do what is recommended, and suffer from other legal
restrictions. Thus they do what they do not wish to
do to save themselves from a worse evil, and not at all
because stockholders, directors or officers suffer particularly because public opinion is against them.

Railroad managers have seen the establishment of railroad commissions with much apprehension, which in several cases has been justified. Now, however, many of them feel that there is advantage in a commission of the Massachusetts type. They would prefer, perhaps, that there should be no such public supervision, but they have become convinced that the public will in some way hold them under restraint, and they know that many acts indispensable to the economical conduct of railroad transportation are likely to be condemned by the public and to lead to legislation from which the railroads would suffer greatly, unless the public can be satisfied that such acts are just and necessary, as it may be by an intelligent tribunal which investigates the facts.

Any one who has studied the course of railroad legislation in European countries must, we think, come to the conclusion that here as elsewhere the railroads will eventually have to submit to some kind of state supervision. It is idle to argue the question of the advantages or disadvantages of such supervision. It is inevitable, and must be put up with. It therefore becomes of the utmost importance to our railroads that the tribunals which the state or the nation sets up should not possess unreasonable powers, and should be composed of men of character, capable of understanding the questions which they investigate and report upon. No despot in modern times exercises the arbitrary and absolute powers over property rights which have been given to some of our state railroad commissions. But these should not be confounded with those whose power consists chiefly in keeping the public and the legislatures informed of what is good and bad in the management of the railroads.

LAWS OF THE VARIOUS STATES ESTABLISHING RAILROAD COMMISSIONS.

In the following statement of the laws of the various states establishing railroad commissions, the laws of California, Massachusetts and New York have been given more fully than those of some other states for the reasons, as respects California, that the commission in that state is a constitutional body ; as respects Massachusetts, that her law has been comparatively long in force and has been followed in the legislation of other states; as respects New York, that railroad management in that state is exceptionally important to the country at large, because the number of roads traversing the state is so large and their traffic so important.

The reader may understand that all the commissions have tolerably broad powers of subpœnaing witnesses and compelling testimony when needful in the discharge of their duties; also, that generally whenever in the statement naught is said about the compensation of the Commissioners, they are paid salaries at the expense of the state.

ALABAMA.

An act of Feb. 26, 1881, Laws 1881, No. 91, p. 84–96, provides for the appointment of three Commissioners. (Sec. 13). There are the usual qualifications as to who may be a Commissioner. (Sec. 14.) The Commission is to revise all tariffs of charges submitted to it for that purpose by any person or company operating a railroad in this state, and if such rates are allowed they shall append a certificate of approval thereto. (Sec. 15.) It is to hear and investigate complaints and give notice of any changes deemed proper in any tariff of rates. (Sec. 16.) The expenses of the Commission shall be borne by the several railroads, and upon a company's paying its assessed proportion of this tax, and upon the satisfactory evidence that it is prepared to transport passengers and freight with safety, the Auditor shall issue a license to said company to operate the road for one year. (Sec. 18.)

When in the judgment of the Commission it shall appear that repairs are necessary upon any railroad, or any addition to its rolling stock or change in or addition to its houses, or change in its rates is reasonable and expedient for the safety, convenience and accommodation of the public, they shall notify it thereof, and include a report of their proceedings in the annual report to the Legislature. (Sec. 20.)

The Commission shall supervise. and examine the railroads of the state and keep themselves informed as to their condition and management. (Secs. 21, 22.) Persons operating railroads are to make annual reports to the Commissioners in manner prescribed by them. (Sec. 25.)

Any accident attended with serious personal injury is to be reported to the Commissioners within twenty-four hours from its occurrence, and they may investigate the same and embrace an account of their proceedings in their annual report. (Sec. 26.) This yearly report of the Commissioners is to contain such facts as disclose the actual working of the railway system in this state, and such suggestions as may seem to them appropriate. They shall also submit such recommendations as to further legislation as they may deem advisable. (Sec. 28.)

A provision not occurring elsewhere makes it the duty of the Commission to confer with the Commissioners of other states, and with such persons from states having no Commissioners, as the Governors thereof may appoint, for the purpose of agreeing upon draft of statutes, to be submitted to the Legislature of each state, to secure such uniform control of railway transportation in the several states, and from one state into another, as will best subserve the interests of trade and commerce. (Sec. 31.)

By-laws 1883, No. 78, p. 151, the Commission may recommend joint local rates to railroads in this state on freight in all cases where such railroads constitute a combination under one general management. Act. No. 79, Laws 1883, Sec. 5, p. 153, provides for the approval of pooling contracts by the Commission. No. 104, Laws 1883,

p. 178, enacts that any duly proved determination of the board concerning a matter of which it has jurisdiction shall, in any proceeding in the courts of the state, be considered *prima facie* right and proper.

ARKANSAS.

In Arkansas there is, or was, a so-called Railroad Commission, consisting of the Governor, the Secretary of State and the Commissioner of Internal Improvements. Its powers and duties relate to applications for state aids to proposed railroads. Companies desiring aid from the state must lay the facts before the Commissioners ; if they approve the application, the Governor, upon their report, may issue bonds for the amount reported to be proper. This Commission has no important authority over roads in operation except as concerns their fiscal relations with the state. (Sec. 4,971–4,973, seq.)

CALIFORNIA.

The constitution directs the election of three Railroad Commissioners, and defines their general powers and duties, among which are: to establish transportation charges; to examine the records, etc., of the company; to hear and determine complaints against them; to prescribe a uniform system of railroad accounts, and to make annual reports to the Governor of the doings of the board.

The following is the chief provision of the constitution, " The state shall be divided into three districts as nearly equal in population as practicable, in each of which one Railroad Commissioner shall be elected by the qualified electors thereof at the regular gubernatorial elections: whose salary shall be fixed by law, and whose term of office shall be four years, commencing on the first Monday after the first day of January next succeeding their election. Said Commissioners shall be qualified electors of this state and of the district from which they are elected, and shall not be interested in any railroad corporation, or other transportation company, as stockholder, creditor, agent, attorney or employé; and the act of a majority of said Commissioners shall be deemed the act of said Commission. Said Commissioners shall have the power, and it shall be their duty, to establish rates of charges for the transportation of passengers and freight by railroad or other transportation companies, and publish the same from time to time, with such changes as they may make; to examine the books, records, and papers of all railroad and other transportation companies, and for this purpose they shall have power to issue subpœnas and all other necessary process; to hear and determine complaints against railroad and other transportation companies, to send for persons and papers to administer oaths, take testimony, and punish for contempt of their orders and processes, in the same manner and to the same extent as courts of record, and enforce their decisions and correct abuses through the medium of the courts. Said Commissioners shall prescribe a uniform system of accounts to be kept by all such corporations and companies. Any railroad corporation or transportation company which shall fail or refuse to conform to such rates as shall be established by such Commissioners, or shall charge rates in excess thereof, or shall fail to keep thier accounts in accordance with the system prescribed by the Commission, shall be fined not exceeding $20,000 for each offense, and every officer, agent, or employé of any such corporation or company, who shall demand or receive rates in excess thereof, or who shall in any manner violate the provisions of this section, shall be fined not exceeding $5,000, or be imprisoned in the county jail not exceeding one year. In all controversies, civil or criminal, the rates of fares and freights established by said Commission shall be deemed conclusively just and reasonable, and in any action against such corporation or company for damages sustained by charging excessive rates, the plaintiff, in addition to the actual damage, may. in the discretion of the judge or jury, recover exemplary damages. Said Commission shall report to the Governor, annually, their proceedings, and such other facts as may be deemed important. Nothing in this section shall prevent individuals from maintaining actions against any of such companies. The Legislature may, in addition to any penalties herein prescribed, enforce this article by forfeiture of charter or otherwise, and may confer such further powers on the Commissioners as shall be necessary to enable them to perform the duties enjoined on them in this and the foregoing section. The Legislature shall have power, by a two-thirds vote of all the members elected to each house, to remove any one or more of said Commissioners from office, for dereliction of duty, or corruption, or incompetency; and whenever, from any cause, a vacancy in office shall occur in said Commission, the Governor shall fill the same by the appointment of a qualified person thereto, who shall hold office for the residue of the unexpired term, and until his successor shall have been elected and qualified." (Cal. Const., 1879, Art. 12, § 22.)

The counties to compose the several railroad districts, until the Legislature should otherwise prescribe, were temporarily designated. (*Id.*, Art. 12, § 23.)

CONNECTICUT.

The General Statutes of Connecticut provide for the appointment of three Commissioners. By Chap. 145, p. 232, Laws 1877, one of these is to be a lawyer of ten years' standing, one a civil engineer and one a practical business man. Their salaries and expenses are to be paid by a tax levied upon the railroads of the state; they may employ experts to assist them. (Gen. Sta s., Tit. 8, Chap. 1, Pt. 7, pp. 15, 16.) Title 17, Chap. 2, Pt. 9, contains provision to the same effect as Mass. Gen. Stat., 1882, Chap. 112, Sec. 141. Semi-annual examinations of railroads within the state are directed. (Sec. 11, p. 320.)

The board shall notify the company to make all repairs required within a time limited; shall make such rules as to platforms and outbuildings at stations as are for the public interest; may prescribe the time during which any ticket-office shall be open for the sale of tickets, and no company neglecting such order shall receive more than the regular ticket price for fare; shall make necessary orders for compelling companies to furnish comfortable seats for passengers, and for regulating the manner in which companies shall manage their engines and cars at highway crossings; shall direct that suitable warning boards be put up at dangerous crossings; may require companies to maintain a gate across a highway at any crossing, and to provide an agent to open and close the same ; shall, when two roads meet or intersect, at the request of the directors of the company owning either, prescribe rules relative to the exchange of passengers and luggage. (Sec. 12, p. 320.)

They may order gates, flagmen or signals to be provided (Sec. 13, p. 120); may recommend measures conducive to public safety, and report neglect to adopt such measures to the General Assembly (Sec. 14, p. 321); may apply for injunction to restrain persons from exercising any official duty in a corporation which has violated the law, or is conducting its affairs in a dangerous manner. (Sec. 15.)

The Commissioners are to report to each General Assembly suggesting such legislation as they deem proper. (Sec 17.)

They shall prescribe the limits within which land may be taken for railroad purposes. (Sec. 18, p. 32.) The routes of new railroads are to be approved by the Commissioners as to intersections, crossings, etc. (Secs. 26, 28, p. 323); also the location and abandonment of depots (Secs. 48, 51, p. 327). They are to secure to all connecting roads equal facilities. (Sec. 62, p. 324.) Companies must provide bridges connecting the several cars of their trains; these appliances to be approved by the Commissioners. (Sec. 5, p. 350.) As in New York, they are to notify the board of accidents occurring on their roads. (Sec. 80, p. 332, as amended laws, 1881, Chap. X., p. 7.)

GEORGIA.

Three Commissioners, of whom one shall be of experience in law, and one of experience in railroad business, are to be appointed by the Governor, with the advice and consent of the Senate. As elsewhere, employment by or interest in a railroad renders one ineligible for the office.

The Commissioners are required to make for each railroad doing business in this state a schedule of just and reasonable rates, and to revise and change the same as often as necessary; said schedule to be published in some public newspaper and posted in all railway stations. (Code, 1882, Sec. 719, f.) They are to investigate the books of the companies, make personal visitation of their railroad offices for the purpose of examination to ascertain whether the rules and regulations to prevent unjust discriminations, etc., have been complied with. (Sec. 719, *g*.) All agreements between companies as to rates of transportation or as to a division of earnings by competing roads shall be submitted to the Commissioners for their inspection and approval, that just and reasonable rates may be secured, and any agreement not approved by them or providing for charges exceeding the rates fixed shall be illegal and void. (Sec. 719, *h*.) Severe penalties are incurred by violating the rules and regulations prescribed. To recover these, actions are to be instituted by the Commissioners through the Attorney-General or Solicitor-General. (Sec. 719, *i*.) The Commissioners are to make semi-annual reports to the Governor, and recommend such legislation as they may deem advisable. (Sec. 719, *u*.) The railroads are to report to the Commissioners. ' (Sec. 719, *p*.)

ILLINOIS.

Three " Railroad and Warehouse Commissioners " are to be appointed by the Governor with the advice and consent of the Senate. No person is to be chosen who is connected with or interested in any railroad company or warehouse. Every railroad company is to make a yearly report to the Commissioners (Rev. Stat., 1880, pp. 1184-1185, Chap. 114, Secs. 153, 154, 158), and they are in turn to report to the Governor once in each year, or oftener if required, making such suggestions as may seem appropriate to them, and particularly, first, whether in their judgment the railroads can be classified in regard to the rate of fare and freight to be charged upon them, and if so, in what manner; second, whether a classification of freight can also be made, and if so, in what manner. They shall also, at such times as the Governor shall direct, examine any particular subject connected with the condition and management of such railroads and warehouses, and report to him in writing their opinion thereon with their reasons therefor. (Sec. 162.) It is the duty of the Commissioners to examine the condition and management of the railroads of the state. One of their number is to visit each county in which is located a railroad station, at least once in six months, and whenever it shall come to their knowledge, either upon complaint or otherwise, or they shall have reason to believe that any law or laws have been or are being violated, they shall prosecute or cause to be prosecuted all corporations or persons guilty of such violation. (Sec. 163.) The Attorney-General and State's Attorney are to prosecute any suit or proceeding which the Commissioners may direct them to prosecute for violation of any law of the state concerning railroads. (Sec. 169)

IOWA.

In this state one of the three Commissioners shall be a civil engineer. There are essentially the same provisions concerning eligibility as those found in the Illinois statute- The Commissioners are to inspect the equipment and management of each railroad in the state ; are to make semiannual examinations of its bridges, and if they shall deem any unsafe and the company shall neglect after notice to repair such bridges, they are empowered to stop the running of trains over them. (McClain's Stats., Vol. I., p. 365.) As in Illinois, the compani s are to report to the Commissioners and they to the Governor once in each year. (pp. 335, 336.)

This report is to contain such facts, statements and explanations as will disclose the working of the system of railroad transportation in this state, and its relation to the general business and prosperity of the citizens of the state; also certain enumerated statistics of each road. The Commissioners are to report, further, violations of the state laws, failures to comply with the terms of charters ; repairs or changes deemed expedient in the road or rolling stock of any company ; also cases of extortion, unjust discrimi ation in rates, etc., satisfactorily proven to the board as provided by the statute. (pp. 365, 369.)

As in Connecticut and New York, it is enacted that a corporation operating a road upon which an accident occurs shall notify the board thereof. An investigation and report are thereupon t be made to the Governor concerning it. (p. 368.)

KANSAS.

Under the provisions of Chap. 124, p. 186, Laws of 1883, there is to be a board of three Railroad Commissioners elected by the Executive Council. As in other states, they must be neither employed by nor interested in any railroad corporation. (Secs. 1–2.) Their salaries and expenses are to be paid by the railroad companies. (Sec. 4.) They are to have general supervision of all steam railroads in the state, all express companies, sleeping-car companies and corporations doing business as common carriers in the state ; are to inquire into any neglect or violation of the laws of the state by them ; to inspect the equipment and management of railroads with reference to public safety and convenience ; to inform the corporations of any improvements or changes in their roads, rolling stock, depots, etc., deemed expedient ; also to recommend modifications in their rates of transportation adjudged reasonable and proper, and are to incorporate an account of such proceedings in a report to be made by them annually to the Governor. Certain particulars concerning the financial condition and statistics of each railroad in the state are also to be included in this report, as well as such further suggestions as may to the board seem appropriate. (Secs. 5–6.) Each company is to report yearly to the Commissioners. (Sec. 7.) Upon complaint in writing that an unreasonable rate has been charged, the board shall investigate such complaint, and if sustained make a certificate setting forth what is a reasonable charge for the service rendered, which report shall be *prima facie* evidence thereof. (Sec. 11.)

All pooling contracts are prohibited between companies whose roads run in the same general direction. (Sec. 12.) On complaint made by certain city or township authorities, etc., the board shall examine the rates of freight tariff charged by any company, and if it appear that the complaint is well founded, they shall so adjudge and fix upon reasonable rates, which are to be accepted by said company, and any excess upon such charges shall, in all actions brought in any court of justice, be *prima facie* unjust and extortionate. All cases of failure to comply with such recommendations shall be reported to the Governor. (Secs. 14, 18.)

Any person engaged in business other than that of a common carrier is also empowered to own railroad cars, and all companies must receive and transport the same on such terms and rates as may be fixed by the Commissioners. (Sec. 15.)

The right to construct a railroad and to take land by eminent domain may, in certain cases, and with the approval of the board, be exercised by private persons. (Sec. 17.) There are heavy penalties for violating or evading the provisions of this act, these to be sued for by the county attorneys upon the directions of the Commissioners. (Secs. 19, 20.)

KENTUCKY.

Chap. 790, Laws 1881-82, Vol. I., p. 66-73, provides for the creation of a Railroad Commission. Its members are to be appointed by the Governor, by and with the advice and consent of the Senate. (§ 5.) No person is to be chosen who is in the employ of or interested in any railroad company. (§ 6.)

To these Commissioners each company is to furnish yearly a statement of its affairs, specifying between thirty and forty prescribed particulars (§ 9), also answers to any additional interrogatories which they may propound. (§ 10.)

Said Commissioners are to make an annual report to the Governor containing such facts as will disclose the practical workings of the system of railroad transportation in this state, and such suggestions in relation thereto as may to them seem appropriate. (§ 11.) They shall examine into the condition and management of railroads in this state, so far as the same pertain to the relation of such railroads to the public, also whether they comply with the laws of the state, and to prosecute or cause to be prosecuted corporations or persons guilty of such violation. (§ 12.) The Attorney-General and Commonwealth's Attorney are, upon request of the Commissioners, to institute and prosecute all proceedings authorized by this act. (§ 16.)

The Commissioner is also to hear and determine complaints of extortion or discrimination in rates by any railroad corporation, rendering such corporation liable to cert·in penalties therein provided. A copy of the Commissioners' award may, under certain circumstances, be filed with Clerk of the Circuit Court, and execution issued thereon. (§ 19, 1. 2, 3, 4.)

MAINE.

The Governor with the advice of Council shall appoint three Railroad Commissioners : two of these shall be experienced in the construction and management of railroads, and one of them shall be an engineer. (Rev. Stats., Chap. 51, Sec. 71, p. 462.)

The majority of the board are annually to examine the tracks, rolling stock, bridges, viaducts and culverts of all railroads, giving a certificate stating the condition thereof to the Clerk of the corporation. (Sec. 72.) The Commissioners may notify a company to make necessary repairs in its road, and require it to reduce the speed of their trains meanwhile. Such orders are to be enforced through the courts, it being the duty of the Attorney General or the county attorneys to take charge of proceedings therein on being notified so to do by the board. (Secs. 74 and 75.) The Commissioners may also order the immediate stopping of all passenger trains about to run over a road considered by them unsafe, and if said order is not obeyed they shall apply at once for an injunction against the company without notice to it. (Laws of 1874, p. 155, Chap. 218. Sec. 2.)

When connecting railroads cannot agree concerning the transportation of passengers or freight, the Commissioners may, on the application of either of them, examine into the matter and fix the terms, rates, etc., upon which passengers, freight or cars shall be carried over the road of each. (Sec. 76.) Their award shall be returned to the Supreme Judicial Court and accepted, or for good cause recommitted or rejec ed. (Sec. 77.) The Commissioners are to examine into the cause of any serious accident, and include the results of such examination in a report which they are to make annually to the Governor. (Sec. 78.) In this report they are to state such facts as they deem of public interest or such as the Governor may require. (Sec. 72.)

The railroads are to report yearly to the board, and the returns shall be as nearly as possible uniform, as to subject matter, with those required in the other New England States. (Sec. 30 as amended, Laws 1877, Chap. 207, p. 154.)

MASSACHUSETTS.

The Board of Railroad Commissioners consists of three persons appointed by the Governor. No person in the employment of or holding stock in a railroad corporation is eligible for the office of Commissioner. (Pub. Stat, 1882, Chap. 112, Sec. 9.)

The salaries and expenses of the Commissioners are to be borne by the railroads and street railways. (Sec. 12.)

The board shall make an annual report of its doings to the General Court, including such statements, facts and explanations as will disclose the actual working of the system of railroad transportation in its bearing upon the business and prosperity of the commonwealth, and such suggestions as to its general railroad policy or any part thereof, or the condition, affairs, or conduct of any railroad corporation, as may seem to it appropriate.

The board shall have the general supervision of all railroads and railways, and shall examine the same ; and the Commissioners shall keep themselves informed as to the condition of railroads and railways, and the manner in which they are operated with reference to the security and accommodation of the public, and as to the compliance of the several corporations with their charters and the laws of the commonwealth. The provisions of the six following sections shall apply to all railroads and railways, and to the corporations, trustees or others owning or operating the same.

The board, whenever in its judgment any such corporation has violated a law, or neglects in any respects to comply with the terms of the act by which it was created, or with the provisions of any law of the commonwealth, shall give notice thereof in writing to such corporation ; and, if the violation or neglect is continued after such notice, shall forthwith present the facts to the Attorney-General, who shall take such proceedings thereon as he may deem expedient.

The board, whenever it deems that repairs are necessary on any railroad, or that an addition to its rolling stock. or an addition to or change of its stations or station houses, or a change in its rates of fares for transporting freight or passengers. or in the mode of operating its road and conducting its business is reasonable and expedient in order to promote the security, convenience and accommodation of the public, shall, in writing, inform the corporation of the improvements and changes which it considers to be proper, and the report of the proceedings shall be included in the annual report of the board.

Upon the complaint and application of the Mayor and Aldermen of a city or the Selectmen of a town within which any part of a railroad is located, the board shall examine the condition and operation thereof ; and if twenty or more legal voters in a city or town, by petition in writing, request the Mayor and Aldermen or Selectmen to make such complaint and application, and they decline so to do. they shall indorse upon the petition the reason of such non-compliance, and return it to the petitioners, who may within ten days thereafter present it to said board, and the board may thereupon proceed to make such examination in the same manner as if called upon by the Mayor and Aldermen or the Selectmen, first giving to the petitioners and to the corporation reasonable notice in writing of the time and place of entering upon the same. If upon such examination it appears to the board that the complaint is well founded, it shall so adjudge, and shall inform the corporation operating such railroad of its adjudication in the same manner as is provided in the preceding section.

The board shall investigate the causes of any accident on a railroad resulting in loss of life, and of any accident not so resulting, which it may deem to require investigation.

Every railroad corporation shall at all times, on request, furnish to the board any information required by it concerning the condition, management and operation of the road of such corporation, and particularly copies of all leases, contracts and agreements for transportation with express companies or otherwise, to which it is a party, and also with the rates for transporting freight and passengers upon its road and other roads with which its business is connected.

No request or advice of the board shall impair in any manner the legal duties and obligations of a railroad corporation, or its legal liability for the consequences of its acts or of the neglect or mismanagement of any of its agents or servants.

The board shall from time to time in each year examine the books and accounts of all corporations operating railroads or street railways, to see that they are kept in a uniform manner and upon the system prescribed by the board. Statements of the doings and financial condition of the several corporations shall be prepared and published at such times as the board shall deem expedient.

On the application in writing of a director or of any person or persons owning one-fiftieth part of the paid in capital stock of a corporation operating a railroad or street railway, or owning the bonds or other evidences of indebtedness of such corporation equal in amount to one-fiftieth part of its paid in capital stock, the board shall examine the books and the financial condition of said corporation, and shall cause the result of such examination to be published in one or more daily papers in the city of Boston.

The board shall at all times have access to the list of stockholders of every corporation operating a railroad or street railway, and may at any time cause the same to be copied, in whole or in part, for the information of the board or of persons owning stock in such corporation. (Secs. 13–23, Chap. 112.)

Here as in other states having Railroad Commissioners the Commissioners may summon witnesses, administer oaths and take testimony. (Sec. 25.)

The board may fix the route of a railroad in a city or town when the town or city authorities cannot agree with the directors of the railroad concerning it (Sec. 41); and the clerk of the board is to certify that the requirements of the law have been complied with before the articles of association are filed. (Chap. 112. Sec. 44.) It may allow a street railway company to increase its capital stock. (Chap. 113, Sec. 15.) No railroad corporation may locate or construct its road until a sworn estimate of the cost of construction is submitted to the board, and the board is satisfied that a certain amount of the stock has been subscribed and paid in. (Chap. 112, Secs. 85, 86.) No railroad shall be constructed across another at the same grade, nor across navigable waters without the consent of the Commissioners. (Chap. 112, Sec. 118.)

No railroad shall be open for use until the board examines it and certifies that the laws relating to its construction have been observed, and that it appears to be in a safe condition. (Chap. 112, Sec. 141.)

If connecting companies cannot agree as to the periods when nor the times upon which cars of the one shall be drawn over the road of the other, nor as to the manner in which passengers and freight shall be transferred, etc., the board shall, upon the application of either party, determine such matters, and apportion expenses, receipts, etc. (Chap. 112, Sec. 218.)

The board has supervision of the re-location of passenger and freight stations. (Chap. 112, Sec. 157.) It may revise the tariff for the care and carriage of milk, and for the rates therefor. (Chap. 112, Sec. 193.) It may regulate the fares established by street railroad companies, but not so as to reduce their profits below a certain percentage upon the cost of the road. (Chap. 113, Sec. 44.) It may make rules regulating the transportation of explosives, the violation of which subjects to heavy penalties. (Chap. 102, 62.) The board may approve of the use of certain mechanical appliances, and may by written notice revoke such approval. (Chap. 112, Sec. 174.) It may also authorize running through trains on the Lord's day. (Chap. 99, Sec. 15.)

MICHIGAN.

A Commissioner of Railroads is to be appointed by the Governor and the appointment confirmed by the Senate. As in Illinois and Iowa, he must not be disqualified by being interested in or connected with any railroad corporation. (Howell's Stats., Secs. 3,285, 3,286.) Every company is to report to him and he to the Governor yearly, substantially as in Illinois. (Secs. 3,291, 3,294.) He is, however, empowered not only to examine the condition and management of railroads and to employ expert assistants in so doing, but to order repairs, direct the rate of speed of trains passing over dangerous tracks, and even to stop their running altogether, the company becoming liable to heavy penalties for disobeying his orders. (Sec. 3,298.)

There are sections (3,299, 3,300) conferring certain powers to regulate the business of connecting roads, which resemble those of Massachusetts. He may direct a corporation to station flagmen or erect bridges at crossings (Sec. 3,301), and is to prosecute or cause prosecutions to be brought for violation of any law pertaining to railroads (Sec. 3,303). The Attorney-General and county attorneys are to institute any proceedings or suits directed by the Commissioner. (Sec. 3,304.)

It is the duty of the Commissioner to visit each county in which a station is located at least once in each year. (Sec. 3,303.)

He may entertain petitions for railroad facilities, and in certain cases require them to be furnished. (Sec. 3,307.)

There are several minor provisions defining his powers and duties concerning the fences to be maintained by railroad companies, the signals to be used by them, etc. (Secs. 3,303, 3,311.) By a later statute every company is to make a monthly report to him concerning its earnings. (Sec. 3,312 a.)

MINNESOTA.

In this state the Railroad Commissioner is elected by the people, and his duties as defined by General Statute, Chap. 6, Section 69, are to inquire into any neglect or violation of the laws of this state, by any railroad corporation doing business therein or by the officers, agents or employés of any such company, and from time to time carefully to examine and inspect the conditions of each railroad in this state, its equipment and management, with relation to the public safety and convenience ; to examine into and ascertain the pecuniary condition and the manner of financial management of each and every railroad company doing business in this state. The companies are to report to him annually, and he is to make a yearly report to the Governor. containing such facts, statements and explanations as will disclose the workings of the system of railroad transportation in this state, and its rel.tions to the general business and prosperity of the citizens of the state ; also. such suggestions and recommendations in respect t' ereto as may to him seem appropriate. (§§ 70, 71.)

MISSOURI.

It is the duty of the Governor, with the consent of the Senate, to appoint three Railroad Commissioners. There are the usual p ovisions as to eligibility. (Rev. Stat., Sec. 837.) The companies are annually to transmit reports to the Commissioners answering 31 specified interrogatories. (Sec. 841.) The Commissioners may classify certain freight, and are further empowered and authorized to reduce rates on any of said railroads or parts of railroads, either in general or special classes, whenever, in their judgment, it can be. equitably done. (Sec. 842.) The Railroad Commissioners shall, as often as they may deem it necessary, carefully examine the condition of the several railroads of this state. and it shall be the duty of said Railroad Commissioners, whenever they have reasonable grounds to believe—either on complaint or otherwise—that any of the tracks, bridges or other structures of any railroads in this state are in a condition which render any of them dangerous or unfit for the transportation of passengers with reasonable safety, to inspect and examine the same; they may thereupon order necessary repairs, and direct the speed of trains unt l the repairs are made. Heavy penalties are incurred by disobeying the orders of the Commissioners, and in case the disregard of the instructions of the Commissioners shall cause any accident whereby human life shall be lost, or passengers maimed or wounded, the superintendent of the company, and the engineer and conductor in charge of the train, shall severally be deemed guilty of a felony, and on conviction thereof shall be imprisoned in the penitentiary for a period of not less than two or more than ten years; and the Commissioners shall have power wholly to stop the running of passenger trains over such defective track, bridge or other structure; and they are hereby required, in c ise any company fail to repair such , track, bridge or other structure within the time required, to give notice of such fact in some newspaper having a general circulation along the line of said railroad to the traveling public. (Sec. 843.)

The decision of the Commissioners with reference to rates is binding on the companies, and there are penalties imposed for charging higher rates. (Sec. 844.)

NEW HAMPSHIRE.

A Board of Railroad Commissioners consisting of three persons shall be elected at the same time and in the same manner as the Governor. (General laws, Chap. 157, Sec. 1.)

Said b ard shall perform all such duties in relation to the laying out of railroads and the determination of questions relating to railroads as may be required by law. (Sec. 6.)

One of said Commissioners, once at least in each year, without previous notice, and whenever the Governor may require it, shall make personally a full examination into the condition of every railroad and the management of its affairs ; inspect, so far as practicable, all books, records, papers, notes, bonds, and other evidences of debt, and all titles of property, deeds, and bills of sale belonging to its proprietors, and ascertain whether they have performed all their duties to the state and individuals, and whether they have violated any provision of their charters, or of the laws relating to railroad corporations or to railroads. (Sec. 7.)

Said Commissioners shall, as soon as may be, report the result of such examination to the Secretary of State, who shall communicate the same in printed form to the Legisture at their next session. (Sec. 8.)

No person interested in any railroad can be a Commissioner. (Sec. 12.)

NEW JERSEY.

In New Jersey there is a so-called railroad commission, consisting of the State Comptroller, Treasurer and Commissioner of Railroad Taxation. Its powers and duties relate to appraising, for the purposes of taxation, the value of the properties of any railroad company which does not make a return thereof as required by the tax laws. The Commissioner has no important authority over the operation and management of railroads. (Act of April 13, 1876. Revision 1877, p. 1168.)

NEW YORK.

The act of June 16, 1882, Laws 1882, Chap. 353, provides that there shall be in and for the State of New York a Board of Railroad Commissioners, to consist of three persons appointed by the Governor by and with the advice and consent of the Senate.

Said Board of Commissioners shall have power to administer oaths in all matters relating to their duties, and shall have the general supervision of railroads and railways (so far as necessary to enable them to perform the duties and exercise the power imposed and conferred by law), and shall examine the same, and keep themselves informed as to their condition, and the manner in which they are operated, with reference to the security and accommodation of the public, and the compliance of the several corporations with the provisions of their charters and the laws of the state ; it shall also be the duty of said Board of Railroad Commissioners to investigate the causes of any accident on a railroad, resulting in loss of life or injury to person or persons which, in their judgment, shall require investigation, and the result of such investigation shall also be reported upon in the annual report of the Commissioners to the Legislature ; and it is hereby made the duty of the General Superintendent or Manager of each railroad in this state to inform the said board of any such accident immediately after its occurrence. Before proceeding to make any such examination or investigation of the condition or operation of any railroad in this state, or any accident thereon, in accordance with this act, said board shall give reasonable notice to the corporation, person or persons conducting and managing the same, of the time and place of entering upon said examination. And such Board of Railroad Commissioners shall have power, for the purposes provided for in this act, to examine the books and affairs of any railroad company or corporation, or to compel the production of copies of books and papers, subpœna witnesses, administer oaths to them, and compel their attendance and examination, as though such subpœna had issued from a court of record of this state. (Chap. 303, Sec. 4.)

Whenever, in the judgment of the Board of Rail·oad Commissioners, it shall appear that any such corporation has violated any constitutional provision or law, or neglects in any respect or particular to comply with the terms of the act by which it was created, or unjustly discriminates in its charges for services, or usurps any authority not by its act of inc rporation granted, or refuses to comply with the provisions of any of the laws of the state, or with any recommendation of said Board of Commissioners, they shall give notice thereof in writing to such corporation, and if the violation or neglect is continued after such notice. the board may forthwith present the fact to the Attorney-General. who shall take such proceedings thereon as may be necessary for the protection of public interests.

Whenever in the judgment of the said Board of Railroad Commissioners, after a careful personal examination of the same, it shall appear that repairs are necessary upon any railroad within this state, or that any addition to the rolling stock, or any addition to or change of the stations or station houses, or that additional terminal facilities shall be afforded, or that any change in the rates of fare for transporting freight or passengers, or that any change in the mode of operating the road and conducting its business is reasonable and expedient in order to promote the security, convenience and accommodation of the public, the said board shall give notice and information in writing to the corporation of the improvements and changes which they deem to be proper, and shall give such corporation an opportunity for a full hearing thereon ; and if the corporation refuses or neglects to make such repairs, improvements and changes, within a reasonable time after such information and hearing, and shall not satisfy said board that no action is required to be taken by it, the said board shall present the facts in the case to the Attorney-General for his consideration and action ; and shall also report the same facts in a special report or in the annual report of said board to the Legislature. (Chap. 353, Secs. 5, 6.)

Every corporation shall at all times on request furnish necessary information concerning the condition and management of its road, but the Commissioners shall not be bound to give publicity to such information if the public interests do not require it. (Sec. 7.)

The said Board of Railroad Commissioners shall make an annual report to the Legislature of their doings, including such statements, facts and explanations as will disclose the actual working of the system of railroad transportation in its bearing upon the business and prosperity of the state, and such suggestions as to the general railroad policy of the state, or the amendment of its laws, or as to the condition. affairs or conduct of any of the railroad corporations, as may seem to them appropriate. And the said Board of Railroad Commissioners shall be charzed with the duty to recommend and draft for the Legislature such bills as will, in their judgment, protect the people's interest iu and upon the railways of this state. And it shall l kewise be the duty of such Commissioners to take testi-mony upon, and have hearing for and against any proposed change of the law relating to any railway or railways or proposed change of the general law in relation to railways, if requested to do so by the Legislature or by the Committee on Railroads of the Senate or Assembly, or by the Governor, or by any railroad company, or by any incorporated organization representing agricultural or commercial interests in the state, and such Commissioners shall thereupon report their conclusions, in writing, to the Legislature or to such legislative committee, governor, company, or such organization from whom the request to act emanated. (Sec. 9, Chap. 353.)

The Commissioners may prescribe the form of report to be made by railroad corporations. (Sec. 10.) The total annual expense of the Board of Commissioners is to be borne by the railroads of the state. (Sec. 13)

Said Railroad Commissioners shall not, directly or indirectly, solicit or request from, or recommend to, any railroad corporation or any officer, attorney or agent thereof, the appointment of any person or persons to any place or position, nor shall any railroad corporation, its attorney or agent, offer any place, appointment or position or other consideration to such Commissioners, or either of them, nor to any clerk or employé of said Commissioners whatever ; neither shall said Commissioners, nor their Secretary, clerks, agents, employés or experts accept, receive or request any pass, present. gift or gratuity of any kind from any railroad corporation, under penalty of forfeiture of office, and any Commissioner who shall secretly reveal any information gained by him from one railroad company to any other railroad company or person shall be guilty of a misdemeanor. (Sec. 14.)

OHIO.

A Commissioner of Railroads and Telegraphs shall be appointed by the Governor. with the advice and consent of the Senate. No person interested in a railroad company is eligible. (Rev. Stat., 1880, Sec. 245.)

When the Commissioner has reasonable grounds to believe, either on complaint or otherwise, that any of the tracks, bridges, or other structures of any railroad in this state are in a condition which renders them, or any of them, dangerous, or unfit for the transportation of passengers, he shall forthwith inspect and examine the same; and if found to be unfit for the safe transportation of passengers, he may notify the railroad officials to make repairs, etc., may prescribe the rate of speed for trains, or wholly stop the running of passenger trains over the same. Those disobeying his orders are to be severely punished. (Sec. 247.)

When the Commissioner, upon complaint or otherwise, has reason to believe that any railroad company. or any officer, agent, or employé of any railroad company, has violated, or is violating, any of the laws of the state, he shall examine into the matter. (Sec. 248.)

The railroads are to file in the Commissioner's office annual reports giving information as to nearly sixty specified particulars. (Sec. 251.)

Every corporation or company operating a railroad, or

any part of a railroad, within this state, shall, on demand of the Commissioner, furnish him with copies of all leases contracts, and agreements with express, sleeping car, freight, or rolling stock companies, or other companies doing business upon or in connection with such road. (Sec. 256.)

The Commissioner is to be notified of all fatal railroad accidents, and may examine into the cause of the same. (Sec. 257.) The forfeitures and penalties provided for are to be collected by civil actions brought by the county attorneys at the instance of the Commissioner, or of a citizen who will become liable for costs. (Secs. 263, 262.)

The Commissioner shall make to the Governor annually a report of the affairs and condition of all the railroad and telegraph companies having lines in this state, and also of accidents on railroads resulting in injuries to persons, and the circumstances and cause thereof; and he shall include in his report such other information and such suggestions and recommendations as, in his opinion, are of importance to the state.

There are several minor provisions to the effect that he mu t enforce a statute requiring railroads to place movable bridges between passenger cars (Secs. 3347 3350); requiring his approval of all freightways to be constructed, Sec. 3356. and allowing trains of one road to cross another's track without previously stopping, on the company's using certain appliances to be approved by the Commissioner. (Laws 1882, p. 95.)

RHODE ISLAND.

The Governor shall appoint a Railroad Commissioner. (Pub. Stats., Chap. 153, Sec. 1, p. 405.) He is to be notified of any railroad accident within twenty-four hours after the happening thereof. (Sec. 18.) He shall thereupon or upon rumor of such accident repair to the place thereof and inquire into the facts and circumstances connected therewith, and shall without charge furnish to any person injured, or the friends of any person killed, such information as he may obtain. (Sec. 23.) He shall, whenever he shall deem it expedient, personally examine into the proceedings of any railroad corporation . . . established this state, and report to the General Assembly, from time to time, whether such facilities and accommodations as are required by law are furnished, and into all the other acts and doings of any such corporation whereby the rights and privileges of this state or any of its citizens may be affected. (Sec. 27.)

He may, on application of the authorities of any town, and after due hearing, require a company to alter the grade of a highway crossing its road so that said highway shall pass over or under said railroad. Should the company neglect or refuse to obey the decision of the Commissioner, said town authorities may make such alterations and recover all charges and expenses from the corporation. (Secs. 33–34.)

Railroads are to report annually to the Commissioner such facts as he may require. (Sec. 4.) The Commissioner shall. every year, and oftener if he deem it necessary, report to the General Assembly of the state the condition and proceedings of the several railroad corporations, so far as public interest may require the same. (Sec. 29.)

SOUTH CAROLINA.

The Railroad Commissioner shall be elected by a joint vote of the General Assembly. He is not to be interest·d in or connected with any railroad company. (General Statutes, 1882, Sec. 1,451.) He is to have the general supervision of all railroads and railways in this state operated by steam, and shall examine the same and keep himself informed as to their condition and the manner in which they are operated, with reference to the security and accommodation of the public, and the compliance of the several corporations with the provisions of their charters and the laws of the state. Whenever he shall be satisfied that a corporation has neglected to comply with the terms of its charter, or with the provisions of any of the laws of the state, especially in regard to the connections with other railroads, the rates of toll, and the time schedule, he shall give notice thereof in writing to such corporation, and if the violation or neglect is continued after such notice he shall apply an injunection to restrain it from further violation of the law or of its charter. (Sec. 1,456.) He may notify a company to make necessary improvements and changes in its rolling stock, station houses, etc., also reasonable modifications of its rates of transportation, and if the corporations fail to adopt his suggestions, may call upon the Attorney-General to take such legal proceedings as he may deem expedient. (Sec. 1,457.) He is authorized to investigate complaints and report to the General Assembly, or if there be necessity for prompt action, he may take such legal proceedings as may be proper. (Sec. 1,458.)

The Railroad Commissioner shall investigate the causes of any accident on a railroad resulting in loss of life, and of any accident not so resulting, which, in his judgment, shall require investigation.

There are the ordinary provisions for an annual report, which is to be made to the Legislature, with a special report of all accidents and the causes thereof, for the preceding year. (Secs. 1,462, 1,463.)

All pooling contracts are to be submitted to the Commissioner for his approval, so far as they may be affected by any of the provisions contained in this chapter, for securing to all persons just, equal and reasonable facilities for transportation of freight and passengers ; and if the agreements violate any provision of the railroad laws, and are not amended within five days after the parties thereto are notified of the Commissioner's objections, he shall thereupon call upon the Attorney-General to institute proceedings to enforce certain penalties provided.

By an act passed in 1883, the South Carolina Railroad Commissioner is required to establish rates of fare and freight for the railroads of the state, very much as is done in Georgia.

TENNESSEE.

The act establishing the Tennessee Railroad Commission' passed in the spring of 1883, provides for a commission of three persons, to be appointed by the Governor, and to hold office till Jan. 1, 1885 ; their successors to be chosen by the people, and to hold office for two years ; one commissioner to be chosen from West, one from Middle and one from East Tennessee.

No person shall be qualified for a Commissioner who owns stock or is connected with railroads.

The Commission is required to examine and revise tariffs, and to hear and investigate all complaints and take necessary action thereon.

The same law defines railroads as public highways, and prohibits all discrimination against persons, corporations and places ; but contracts for special rates for the purpose of developing industrial enterprises are permitted.

The penalty for extortionate rates. or discrimination in rates, is fixed at ten times the amount of damages, to be recovered by suit brought by the aggrieved party; but if the rates charged have been approved by the Railroad Commission, only actual damage can be recovered. The Attorney-General, on information of the Railroad Commission, must bring suit for any violation of the law. The approval of the Railroad Commission is *prima facie* evidence of the reasonableness of the rates. Rates shall not be deemed extortionate if it can be shown that the net earnings of a road do not exceed a fair interest on its value as assessed for taxation. Tariffs must be posted at all stations.

Contracts for division of business or for buying off competition are prohibited, and railroads are required to receive all business offered to the extent of their facilities ; provided that free transportation is not prohibited unless offered to evade this law.

The law requires the Commission to inspect railroads and require the companies to make such changes, repairs, etc., as may be necessary for proper conduct of business. The railroad companies must pass commissioners free and give them all necessary facilities for inspection. The commissioners to have general supervision over the railroads and to keep themselves informed as to their condition, methods of operating, etc. To investigate all accidents, with authority to summon witnesses, and to make a report to the Legislature yearly.

The Commission has the right to examine stock books of companies, and is to confer with commissioners of other states, with a view to securing uniformity of laws relating to railroads.

One peculiar section of this law, doubtless intended to meet the objection that restrictive legislation would check railroad construction, provides that "none of the provisions of this act shall apply to any railroad now being constructed, or which may hereafter be begun and constructed in this state, until 10 years after the completion of such new railroad."

VERMONT.

The Senate and House of Representatives are to elect a Railroad Commissioner, who must not be a stockholder, officer, trustee, assignee or lessee of any railroad. (Rev. Laws, sec. 3,481.)

The Commissioner shall inquire into, examine and report biennially to the Governor.

Any neglect or infringement of the laws for the regulation of railroads by officers, employés or agents of such roads.

The condition of each railroad, its state of repair and its conduct and management for the public safety.

The causes of the failure of proper railroad connections, if there has been any, and wherein such failure consists.

The pecuniary condition and financial management of the railroads for each of the two preceding years (Sec. 3482); also cases wherein a company has exceeded its powers or incurred a forfeiture of its franchises, that proceedings may be taken therefor. He shall also report what further legal provision should, in his opinion, be adopted in relation to railroads. (Sec. 3,483.)

The Commissioner may establish a uniform system of keeping railroad accounts, and of making and publishing returns of the condition of railroads, so as to conform, as far as practicable, to a uniform system, adopted by the states of Maine, Massachusetts, New Hampshire, Rhode Island, Connecticut and New York. (Sec. 3,484.)

The management of each railroad shall make to the Commissioner under oath such returns and in such form and at such time as he prescribes and makes known to them. (Sec. 3486.) His salary and expenses are to be taxed upon the railroad companies. (Sec. 3,491.) He is to prosecute for certain offenses to bridges and ladders or steps of cars. (Secs. 3,418-3,421.)

VIRGINIA.

Chap. 254, Laws 1876-7, provides that there shall be a Railroad Commissioner to be elected by the General Assembly. He must not be employed by or interested in any railroad in this or any other state. (Sec. 1.) Said Commissioner is to have the general supervision of all railroads in the state operated by steam, is to examine them and keep himself informed as to their physical condition, and the manner in which they are operated, with reference to the security and accommodation of the public, and also as to the compliance of the companies with tl e provisions of the charters and of the laws. (Sec. 2.)

Whenever it shall appear in the judgment of the Commissioner that a company has neglected to comply with the terms of its charter or the provisions of the laws of the state, especially concerning connections with other railroads, the rates of toll and the time schedule, he shall give notice thereof to such corporations, and if the violation of neglect is continued, report the facts to the Board of Public Works, and such board, if on inquiry it seems proper or necessary, shall direct the Commissioner to apply for an injunction to restrain further continuance of said unlawful acts. (Sec. 3.) He may inform a corporation of repairs, additions, etc., deemed reasonable and expedient for the security and convenience of the public, and on its failure to adopt his requirements report the facts to the Board of Public Works for its action. (Section 4.)

Upon complaint of certain city, county or town authorities, he may examine the physical condition of any road, and if the complaint appears on investigation well founded, may notify the company thereof, and on its failure to remove the cause of the complaint, inform the Board of Public Works of his proceedings, etc. (Sec. 5.)

Annual returns are to be made to the Commissioner by the companies (Sec. 10), and they are at all times to furnish him with such information concerning the physical condition of their roads as he may require. (Sec. 7.)

The Commissioner is to report annually to the Legislature such statements, facts, etc., as will disclose the actual woiking of the system of railroad transportation in its bearings upon the business and prosperity of the state— such suggestions as to the general policy of the commonwealth as may seem appropriate, with a special report of all accidents and the causes thereof for the preceding year. (Sec. 9.)

He is to investigate the cause of railroad accidents. (Sec. 6.)

He is to employ experts when necessary. (Secs. 11, 13.)

The railroad companies are to bear the expenses of the Commission. (Sec. 12.)

Chap. 234, Laws 1877-8, Amended Laws 1878-9, p. 367, provide that the Commissioner shall contract with the several railroad companies doing business in the state for the transportation of convicts and lunatics, with their attendants.

Laws 1878-9, p. 256, enact that it shall be the Commisuioner's duty to cause to be printed and posted at each railroad station such portions of the statutes regulating the tolls of the railroads and otherwise prescribing their duties as may seem proper to the Commissioner, together with such explanations and suggestions as will inform the public of their rights, and enable any person who may complain of any violation of such statutes to have such violation properly inquired into and punished.

WISCONSIN.

The Governor, by and with the advice and consent of the Senate, shall appoint a Railroad Commissioner, who is not to be a person employed by or interested in any railroad. freight or transportation company. (Rev. Stats., Secs. 1,792-1,793.)

Such Commissioner shall inquire into any neglect or violation of the laws of the state by any railroad corporation doing business therein, or by the officers, agents or employés thereof, or by any person operating a railroad. He shall inspect and examine the condition, equipment and manner of management of all railroads, with relation to the public safety and convenience. He shall also examine and ascertain the pecuniary condition and the manner of the financial management of every such railroad corporation. Whenever he shall receive any complaint in writing, made by any citizen of this state, of any such neglect or violation of law, and specifying the acts complained of, such Commissioner shall investigate the same ; and if he shall find such complaint well founded he may, in his discretion, report the facts to the Attorney-General, who shall thereupon prosecute an action thereon in the name of and for the benefit of the party aggrieved, at the expense of the state. (Sec. 1,794.)

The Commissioner is to ascertain from each company, through returns which they are required to make to him, certain facts concerning their receipts, earnings, indebtedness, etc. These are to be forwarded to the State Treasurer ; he is also, annually, to make a report to the Governor of the transactions of his office for the preceding year, and containing such information, suggestions or recommendations in respect to the matters under his charge, as he may deem proper. (Sec. 1,795.)

Section 1,797, as amended, laws of 1881, Chap. 224, page 269, allows him when necessary to employ experts to assist him in examining bridges.

www.ingramcontent.com/pod-product-compliance
Lightning Source LLC
Chambersburg PA
CBHW020240090426
42735CB00010B/1781